ITALIAN
FOR BEGINNERS

Angela Wilkes
Illustrated by John Shackell

Designed by Roger Priddy
Edited by Nicole Irving
Language Consultants: Patrizia Di Bello & Giorgio Chiosso

CONTENTS

Handlettering by Jack Potter

About this book

Going abroad is much more fun if you can speak a little of the language. This book shows you that learning another language is a lot easier than you might think. It teaches you the Italian you will find useful in everyday situations.

You can find out how to . . .

talk about yourself,

and your home,

count and tell the time,

say what you like,

find your way around

and ask for what you want in shops.

How you learn

Picture strips like this show you what to say in each situation. Read the speech bubbles and see how much you can understand by yourself, then look up any words you do not know. Words and phrases are repeated again and again, to help you remember them.

The book starts with really easy things to say and gets more difficult towards the end.

New words

All the new words you come across are listed on each double page, so you can look them up as you go along. If you forget any words you can look them up in the glossary on pages 46-48. *If you see an asterisk by a word, it means that there is a note about it at the bottom of the page.

Grammar

Boxes like this around words show where new grammar is explained. You will find Italian easier if you learn some of its grammar, or rules, but don't worry if you don't understand it all straightaway. You can look up any of the grammar used in the book on pages 42-43.

How to say things

On page 41 you can find out how to pronounce the different letters in Italian. The best way to find out how to pronounce words though is to ask an Italian friend.

Puzzles

All the way through the book there are puzzles and quizzes to help you practise your Italian and test yourself. You can check whether your answers are right on pages 44-45.

Practising your Italian

Write all the new words you learn in a notebook and try to learn a few every day. Keep going over them and you will soon remember them.

Ask a friend to keep testing you on your Italian. Even better, ask someone to learn Italian with you so that you can practise on each other.

Vorrei . . .

Try to go to Italy for your holidays, and speak as much Italian as you can. Don't be afraid of making mistakes. No one will mind.

Saying "Hello and Goodbye"

The first thing you should know how to say in Italian is "Hello". There are different greetings for different times of day. Here you can find out what to say when.

In Italy it is more polite to add **signora** or **signorina** when you greet a woman or a girl you don't know. The word for a man is **signore** but you don't often use it.

Saying "Hello"

This is how to say "Hello" to your friends.

This is more polite and means "Have a good day".

This is how you say "Good evening" to someone.

Saying "Goodbye"

Ciao can mean "Goodbye" as well as "Hello".

These are different ways of saying "See you again".

Saying "Goodnight"

You only say **Buona notte** last thing at night.

4

How are you?

This is how to greet someone and ask how they are.

This person is saying that she is fine, thank you...

... but this one is saying things aren't too good.

Come stai?

This list shows you different ways of saying how you are, from very well to terrible. What do you think each of the people here would say if you asked them how they were?

molto bene	very well
bene	well
benino	quite well
non molto bene	not very well
molto male	terrible

5

What is your name?

Here you can find out how to ask someone their name and tell them yours, and how to introduce your friends. Read the picture strip and see how much you can understand. Then try doing the puzzles on the page opposite.

New words

io*	I
tu*	you
lui*	he
lei*	she
loro*	they
come ti chiami (tu)?	what are you called?
come si chiama (lui/lei)?	what is he/she called?
come si chiamano (loro)?	what are they called?
io mi chiamo	I am called
lui si chiama	he is called
lei si chiama	she is called
loro si chiamano	they are called
chi è lui/lei?	who is he/she?
chi è quello /quella?	who is that? (male/female)
questo/questa è	this is (m/f)
il mio amico	my friend (m)
la mia amica	my friend (f)
e tu?	and you?
sì	yes
no	no

Chi è?

In Italian to ask "who is that?", "who is he/she?", "who is it?" or even "who is who?" you can simply ask **chi è?**

Buongiorno, come ti chiami?

Dario, e tu?

Io mi chiamo Monica.

Introducing friends

Questo è un mio amico. Si chiama Piero.

Chi è lei?

Lei è una mia amica. Si chiama Maria.

Come si chiamano?

Loro si chiamano Paolo e Gianni.

*In Italian these words are often left out.

What are they called?

Can you answer these questions in Italian?

Who is who?

Can you answer the questions below the picture?

Who is talking to Gianni?
Who is talking to Valeria?

Who is called Michele?
Who is talking to him?

Who is called Anna?
Who is going home?

Can you remember?

How would you ask someone their name?
How would you tell them your name?

You have a friend called Valeria. How would you introduce her to someone?
How would you tell someone your friend is called Daniele?

Finding out what things are called

Everything on this picture has its name on it. See if you can learn the names for everything, then try the memory test at the bottom of the opposite page. You can find out what **il**, **lo**, **l'** and **la** mean in the box below the picture.

il comignolo

il tetto

il sole

l' uccello

il nido

Buon-giorno!

l' albero

la finestra

il fiore

la casa

Questa è la mia casa.

il garage

la porta

lo steccato

il cane

il gatto

la macchina

Il, lo, l' and la words

Italian nouns are masculine or feminine. The word for "the" shows the gender: **Il** (or **lo**) before masculine (m) nouns, **la** before feminine (f) ones and **l'** before all nouns starting with a vowel.* "A" or "an" is **un** before **il** and masculine **l'** words (**uno** before **lo** words), **una** before **la** words, **un'** before feminine **l'** words.

il sole	sun	**il garage**	garage	**lo steccato**	fence
il tetto	roof	**il fiore**	flower	**la casa**	house
il gatto	cat	**il comignolo**	chimney	**la finestra**	window
il cane	dog	**l' albero (m)**	tree	**la porta**	door
il nido	nest	**l' uccello (m)**	bird	**la macchina**	car

*Always learn which word to use with each noun.

Asking what things are called

Don't worry if you don't know what something is called in Italian. To find out what it is, just ask someone **che cos'è?** Look at the list of useful phrases below, then read the picture strip to see how to use them.

che cos'è?	what is it?
questo è . . .	this is . . . (m)
questa è . . .	this is . . . (f)
anche	also
in italiano	in Italian
in inglese	in English

Che cos'è?

Un fiore.

Anche questo è un fiore?

No, questo è un albero.

Che cos'è in italiano?

Questa è una porta.

E questo cos'è?

Questo è un cane.

Che cos'è in inglese?

A dog!

Can you remember?

Cover up the opposite page and see if you can name these things in Italian. Don't forget to say whether they are **il**, **lo**, **l'** or **la** words.

Where do you come from?

Here you can find out how to ask people where they come from. You can also find out how to ask if they speak Italian.

New words

da* dove vieni?	where do you come from?
io vengo da . . .	I come from . . .
dove abiti?	where do you live?
io abito a . . .	I live in (town)
io abito in . . .	I live in (country)
tu parli . . ?	do you speak . . ?
io parlo	I speak . . .
un poco	a little
italiano	Italian
inglese	English
tedesco	German
ecco	here is
noi	we
voi	you (plural)

Countries

l'Italia (f)	Italy
la Germania	Germany
l' Inghilterra (f)	England
la Francia	France
l' India (f)	India
la Scozia	Scotland
l' Austria (f)	Austria
la Spagna	Spain
l' Ungheria (f)	Hungary

Where do you come from?

Do you speak Italian?

*Da means "from". Dalla means "from the" (feminine); it changes to dall' before a feminine word beginning with a vowel: Io vengo dall' Inghilterra (I come from England).

Who comes from where?

These are the contestants for an international dancing competition. They have come from all over the world. The compère does not speak any Italian and does not understand where anyone comes from. Read about the contestants, then see if you can tell him what he wants to know. His questions are beneath the picture.

Angus viene dalla Scozia.

Ecco Marie e Pierre. Loro vengono dalla Francia.

Hari e Indira vengono dall' India.

Yuri viene dall' Ungheria. Abita a Budapest.

Franz viene dall' Austria.

Where do they all come from?

Ecco Lolita. Lei viene dalla Spagna.

Where does Franz come from?
What are the Indian contestants called?
Is Lolita Italian or Spanish?

Is there a Scottish contestant?
Where do Marie and Pierre come from?
Who lives in Budapest? Where is Budapest?

Verbs (action words)	**parlare**	to speak	**venire**	to come
Italian verbs change according to who is doing the action. Verbs ending in **are** follow the same pattern and have the same endings as **parlare**. You will have to learn **venire** by itself.*	**io parlo** **tu parli** **lui/lei parla** **noi parliamo** **voi parlate** **loro parlano**	I speak you speak he/she speaks we speak you speak (pl) they speak	**io vengo** **tu vieni** **lui/lei viene** **noi veniamo** **voi venite** **loro vengono**	I come you come he/she comes we come you come (pl) they come

Can you remember?

How would you ask someone where they come from?

Can you say where you come from?
How do you say that you speak Italian?
How would you ask someone if they can?

*You can find out more about verbs on pages 42-43.

More about you

Here you can find out how to count up to 20, say how old you are and say how many brothers and sisters you have.

To say how old you are in Italian, you say how many years you have. So if you are ten, you say **io ho dieci anni** (I have ten years).

New words

quanti anni hai?	How old are you?
io ho cinque anni	I am five years old
tu hai . . ?	have you . . ?
io ho	I have
io non ho	I have no
nessun(o) /nessuna	not any
il fratello	brother
la sorella	sister
quasi	almost
né	nor
ma	but

Plural words

Italian nouns and the word for "the" change when you are talking about more than one thing. Masculine words: **il** becomes **i**, **lo** and **l'** become **gli**, and the final letter changes to **i**. Feminine words: **la** and **l'** become **le**, and the final **letter** changes to **e**.*

Numbers**

1	uno	11	undici
2	due	12	dodici
3	tre	13	tredici
4	quattro	14	quattordici
5	cinque	15	quindici
6	sei	16	sedici
7	sette	17	diciassette
8	otto	18	diciotto
9	nove	19	diciannove
10	dieci	20	venti

How old are you?

Have you any brothers and sisters?

*You can read about plurals on pages 42-43.   **You will find a complete list of numbers on page 40.

How old are they?

Read what these children are saying, then see if you can say how old they all are.

Giulio ha dodici anni.

Noi abbiamo quindici anni.

Paola ha undici anni.

Michele ha quasi quattordici anni.

Io ho cinque anni. Lui ha nove anni.

Michele   Diana e Silvia   Giulio   Paola   Luca   Lisa

How many brothers and sisters?

Below you can read how many brothers and sisters the children have. Can you work out who has which brothers and sisters?

Diana e Silvia hanno un fratello e due sorelle.

Paola ha tre sorelle e due fratelli.

Michele ha cinque sorelle, ma nessun fratello.

Luca ha un fratello, ma nessuna sorella.

Giulio non ha fratelli né sorelle, ma ha un cane.

Useful verbs

avere	to have		essere*	to be
io ho	I have		io sono	I am
tu hai	you have		tu sei	you are
lui/lei ha	he/she/it has		lui/lei è	he/she/it is
noi abbiamo	we have		noi siamo	we are
voi avete	you have (pl)		voi siete	you are (pl)
loro hanno	they have		loro sono	they are

*Essere is used on the next page, so it may help you to learn it now.

Talking about your family

On these two pages you will learn lots of words which help you to talk about your family. You will also find out how to say "my" and "your" and describe people.

Ecco la mia famiglia.

il mio cane

mio nonno

mia nonna

mio padre

mia madre

mia sorella

mio fratello

mio zio

mia zia

il mio gatto

Who's who?

Questo è tuo fratello?

Sì, è mio fratello.

E questa, è tua sorella?

Sì, si chiama Ilaria.

Sono i tuoi genitori?

No! Sono i miei nonni.

New words

la famiglia	family	**la zia**	aunt	**magro/magra**	thin
il nonno	grandfather	**i nonni**	grandparents	**vecchio/vecchia**	old
la nonna	grandmother	**i genitori**	parents	**giovane (m and f)**	young
il padre	father	**alto/alta**	tall	**biondo/bionda**	blond
la madre	mother	**basso/bassa**	small/short	**castano/castana**	chestnut brown
lo zio	uncle	**grasso/grassa**	fat	**affettuoso/a**	friendly

How to say "my" and "your"

When you say "my" or "your" in Italian, you don't usually drop the word for "the", e.g. **la mia famiglia** (my family).

"My" and "your" also change depending on whether you are talking about a masculine, feminine or plural word.*

	my	your
il words	**(il) mio****	**(il) tuo****
la words	**(la) mia**	**(la) tua**
i plurals	**(i) miei**	**(i) tuoi**
le plurals	**(le) mie**	**(le) tue**

*You can find out more about this on pages 42-43.
Before **mio and **tuo** you use **il**, even if it is a **lo** word, e.g. **lo steccato**, **il mio steccato** (the fence, my fence).

Describing your family

> Mio padre è alto e mia madre è bassa.

> Mia madre è alta e mio padre è basso.

> Mio zio è grasso e mia zia è magra.

> I miei nonni sono vecchi. Io sono giovane.

> Mia sorella è bionda. Mio fratello è castano.

> Il mio cane è affettuoso.

Describing words

Italian adjectives change their endings depending on whether they are describing a masculine or feminine word. In the word list both forms are shown. Usually the **o** at the end of the masculine form changes to **a** in the feminine, e.g. **alto**, **alta**.*

Can you describe each of these people in Italian, starting **Lui è …** or **Lei è …?**

*You can find out more about adjectives on pages 42-43.

15

Your home

Here you can find out how to say what sort of home you live in and whereabouts it is. You can also learn what all the rooms are called.

New words

o	or
la casa	house
l'appartamento (m)	flat
il castello	castle
in città*	in the town
in campagna	in the country
in riva al mare	by the sea
babbo (or papà)	Dad
mamma	Mum
nonno	Grandad
nonna	Granny
il fantasma	ghost
dove siete?	where are you? (pl)
il bagno	bathroom
la stanza da pranzo	dining room
la stanza da letto	bedroom
il soggiorno	living room
la cucina	kitchen
l' ingresso (m)	hall
il piano di sopra	upstairs

Where do you live?

Tu abiti in una casa o in un appartamento?

Io abito in una casa.

Io abito in un appartamento.

Io abito in un castello.

Town or country?

Io abito in città.

Io abito in campagna.

Io abito in riva al mare.

*In means "in". It becomes nel, nello before il, lo words; nella before la words; nell' before l' words.

Where is everyone?

Babbo comes home and wants to know where everyone is. Look at the pictures and see if you can tell him where everyone is, e.g. **Nonna è** **nel soggiorno**. Then see if you can answer the questions below the little pictures.

mamma   babbo   nonno

nonna   Piero   Isabella

Simone   il fantasma

Chi è nella stanza da pranzo?
Chi è in cucina?
Chi è in bagno?
Chi è nella stanza da letto?

Dov'è mamma?
Dov'è il fantasma?
Dov'è il cane?
Dov'è Piero?
Dov'è babbo? (Look at the word list)

Sono al piano di sopra!

Io sono in bagno.

Io sono nella stanza di Isabella.

Io sono nel soggiorno.

Io sono nella stanza da letto.

Dove siete?

Io sono nella stanza da pranzo.

Io sono in cucina.

Can you remember?

How do you ask someone where they live?
How do you ask whether they live in a house or a flat?

Can you remember how to say "in the country"?
Can you remember how to say "in the town"?

How would you tell someone you were upstairs?
How would you tell them you were in the kitchen?

Looking for things

Here you can find out how to ask someone what they are looking for and tell them where things are. You can also learn lots of words for things around the house.

New words

cercare	to look for
qualcosa	something
il criceto	hamster
trovare	to find
lo	him/it
sopra	on
sotto	under
dietro	behind
davanti a	in front of
tra	between
a fianco a	next to
il mobile	cupboard
l' armadio (m)	wardrobe
la poltrona	armchair
la tenda	curtain
la pianta	plant
lo scaffale	shelf
la tavola	table
il tappeto	carpet
il divano	sofa
la televisione	television
il telefono	telephone
il vaso	vase
eccolo!	there it/he is!

He, she, it

When you are talking about things in Italian, the verb alone makes clear what you are talking about, and you don't use any word for "it":

Dov'è il telefono?
È sulla tavola.

It is the same when you are talking about people or pets: although there are words for "he" and "she" – **lui** and **lei**, you usually use the verb on its own.

The missing hamster

Cerchi qualcosa?

Cerco il mio criceto. Non lo trovo!

Non è sopra l'armadio.

Non è sotto il divano.

È dietro la tenda?

No.

Eccolo! Tra le piante!

18

In, on or under?

Try to learn these words by heart. With **davanti al**, **a fianco al**, **al** changes to **allo** before a **lo** word, **alla** before a **la** word and **all'** before a word beginning with a vowel.

dentro

dietro

davanti a

a fianco a   *sotto*

sopra

Where are they hiding?

Signor Bianchi's six pets are hiding somewhere in the room, but he cannot find them. Can you tell him where they are in Italian, using the words above?

il criceto

il gatto

il cane

il pappagallo

il serpente

la tartaruga

lo scaffale

il vaso

il mobile

la televisione

il telefono

il tappeto

la tavola

la poltrona

il divano

What do you like eating?

Here you can find out how to say what you like and don't like.

New words

mi piace	I like
ti piace?	do you like?
non mi piace*	I don't like
cosa . . ?	what . . ?
amare	to love
non . . . affatto	not at all
allora	then
molto	a lot
di più	more/the most
io preferisco	I prefer
soprattutto	above all
l' insalata (f)	salad
il pesce	fish
le patate fritte	chips
la torta	cake
le salsicce	sausages
gli spaghetti	spaghetti
mangiare	to eat
la pizza	pizza
l' amburgher (m)	hamburger
il riso	rice
il pane	bread
il formaggio	cheese
anche a me	(to) me too

What do you like?

Ti piace l'insalata?

No, non mi piace l'insalata.

Ti piace il pesce?

No, non mi piace affatto.

Cosa ti piace, allora?

Mi piacciono le patate fritte.

E amo le torte!

What do you like best?

Cosa ti piace di più?

Mi piacciono molto le salsicce.

...Ma preferisco la pizza.

...E soprattutto amo molto gli spaghetti!

*You can read more about negatives on pages 42-43.

What are they eating?

Cosa mangi?

Io mangio una pizza.

Lei mangia delle * patate fritte.

Lui mangia del pane e formaggio.

Noi mangiamo degli amburgher.

Voi mangiate del riso.

Loro mangiano delle banane.

Who likes what?

Who likes cheese? Who doesn't like ham?
Who prefers grapes to bananas?

Can you say in Italian which things you like
and which you don't like?

Anche a me, ma non mi piace il prosciutto.

Gianni

Mi piace il formaggio.

Diego

Mi piacciono le banane.

Simone

Io preferisco l'uva.

nonno

Mi piace soprattutto la crostata di frutta.

Isabella

il prosciutto   il burro   la pizza

il pane

l'insalata   i pomodori   il formaggio

le banane   l'uva   una crostata di frutta   il succo d'arancia

---

Mi piace, mi piacciono

Where in English we say "I like", the Italians
say "(it) pleases me": **mi piace** or

"(they) please me": **mi piacciono**.

mi piace/piacciono	I like
ti piace/piacciono	you like

---

*Del, **dello** etc. can mean "some", so **Lei mangia delle patate fritte** means "She is eating some chips". You can
read more about this on page 42.

Table talk

Here you can learn all sorts of useful things to say if you are having a meal with Italian friends.

New words

a tavola, è pronto	come to the table, it's ready
ho fame	I am hungry
anche io	me too
serviti	help yourself
servitevi	help yourselves
buon appetito	enjoy the meal
grazie, altrettanto	thank you, and you too
mi puoi passare . . .	can you pass me . . .
l' acqua (f)	water
il pane	bread
il bicchiere	glass
lei vuole . . ?*	would you like . . ?
ancora	more
la carne	meat
sì, grazie	yes, please
no, grazie	no, thanks
è abbastanza	I've had enough
è buono?	is it good?
è delizioso	it's delicious

Dinner is ready

A tavola, è pronto!

Ho fame.

Anche io!

Prego, serviti!

Grazie.

Buon appetito!

Grazie, altrettanto!

Please will you pass me . . .

Mi puoi passare l'acqua, per favore?

Mi puoi passare il pane, per favore?

Mi puoi passare un bicchiere, per favore?

*Lei is a polite way of saying "you". You can find out more about it on page 23.

Would you like some more?

Who is saying what?

These little pictures show you different things that can happen at mealtime.

Cover up the rest of the page and see if you can say what everyone would say in Italian.

Simone is saying he is hungry.

The chef wants you to enjoy your meal.

Isabella is saying "Help yourself".

Piero wants someone to pass him a glass.

Nonna is offering Simone more chips.

He says "Yes please" and that he likes chips.

Then he says "No thanks. That's enough."

Marco is saying the food is delicious.

Lei

Lei is used as a polite way of saying "you", for example to somebody you don't know. With **lei**, the verb follows the "she" form (whether you are talking to a man or a woman), e.g. **Signore, lei vuole ancora carne? Signora, lei vuole ancora patate fritte?**

23

Your hobbies

These people are talking about their hobbies.

New words

fare	to do/make
dipingere	to paint
cucinare	to cook
tempo libero	spare time
fare del modellismo	to build models
ballare	to dance
leggere	to read
guardare la televisione	to watch TV
lavorare a maglia	to knit
nuotare	to swim
giocare	to play
lo sport	sport
il calcio	football
il tennis	tennis
la musica	music
ascoltare	to listen to
suonare	to play (music)
lo strumento	instrument
il violino	violin
il pianoforte	piano
di sera	in the evening

---

fare (to make or do)

io faccio	I do
tu fai	you do
lui/lei fa	he/she does
noi facciamo	we do
voi fate	you do (pl)
loro fanno	they do

giocare and suonare

When you talk about playing a sport or a game, you say **giocare a**, then the name of the sport, e.g. **gioco a calcio**. (I play football).

To talk about playing an instrument, you say **suonare**, e.g. **suono il pianoforte** (I play the piano).

What do you do in the evenings?

24

The sporty type

Music lovers

What are they doing?

Cover up the rest of the page and see if you can say what all these people are doing in Italian, e.g. **Lui gioca a calcio.** What are your hobbies?

*Degli here means "any". You can read more about this on pages 42-43.

Telling the time

Here you can find out how to tell the time in Italian. You can look up any numbers you don't know on page 40.

There is no word for "past" in Italian. To say "past five" you say **e cinque** (and five); to say "five to" you say **meno cinque** (minus five), after the hour: **sono le nove meno cinque** (it is five to nine).

What is the time?

Here is how to ask what the time is.

New words

che ore sono?	what is the time?
è l'una	it is one o'clock
sono le due	it is two o'clock
meno cinque	five to
e un quarto	quarter past
meno un quarto	quarter to
e mezza*	half past
mezzanotte	midnight
mezzogiorno	midday
del mattino	in the morning
della sera	in the evening
all' una	at one
alle due	at two
alzarsi	to get up
fare colazione	to have breakfast
il pranzo	lunch
la cena	supper, dinner
lui va	he goes
a scuola	to school
a letto	to bed

andare (to go)

io vado	I go
tu vai	you go
lui/lei va	he/she goes
noi andiamo	we go
voi andate	you go (pl)
loro vanno	they go

The time is . . .

Sono le nove e cinque.

Sono le nove e un quarto.

Sono le nove e mezza.

Sono le dieci meno un quarto.

Sono le dieci meno cinque.

È mezzogiorno/ mezzanotte.

What time of day?

Sono le sei del mattino.

Sono le sei della sera.

*To say "half past twelve" you say **mezzanotte/mezzogiorno e mezza.**

Marco's day

Read what Marco does throughout the day, then see if you can match each clock with the right picture. You can find out what the answers are on pages 44-45.

a   b   c   d   e   f   g   h

1

Marco si alza alle sette e mezza.*

2

Fa colazione alle otto.

3

Alle nove meno un quarto va a scuola.

4

Mangia il pranzo a mezzogiorno e mezza.

5

Alle due e dieci gioca a calcio.

6

Alle cinque e un quarto guarda la televisione.

7

Mangia la cena alle sei.

8

E va a letto alle otto e mezza.

What time is it?

Can you say in Italian what times these clocks show?

---

*Some verbs are formed from two parts. You can read about these on pages 42-43.

27

Arranging things

Here is how to arrange things with your friends.

New words

andiamo . . ?	shall we go . . ?
quando?	when?
martedì	Tuesday
di mattina	in the morning
di pomeriggio	in the afternoon
di sera	in the evening
la piscina	swimming pool
verso	at about
a martedì	until Tuesday
oggi	today
ci vediamo	see you
domani	tomorrow
stasera	this evening
va bene	O.K.
non posso	I can't
che peccato!	what a pity!
andare a /in	to go to
il cinema	cinema
la festa	party

Days of the week

la domenica	Sunday
il lunedì	Monday
il martedì	Tuesday
il mercoledì	Wednesday
il giovedì	Thursday
il venerdì	Friday
il sabato	Saturday

Tennis

Swimming

Going to the cinema

Going to a party

Your diary for the week

Here is your diary, showing you what you are doing for a week. Read it, then see if you can answer the questions at the bottom of the page in Italian.

Lunedì
Tennis alle 4.

Martedì
Pianoforte alle 2.
5.30 Piscina.

Mercoledì
Tennis alle 3.
7.45 Al cinema.

Giovedì

Venerdì
Vado a ballare con Diego, alle 8.

Sabato
Calcio alle 2.
7 Festa.

Domenica
Tennis nel pomeriggio.

Che cosa fai venerdì?
Quando giochi a tennis?
Quando vai al cinema?
Quando suoni il pianoforte?
Che cosa fai domenica?*
A che ora è la festa, sabato?**

a
A means to, at: **al cinema** (to/at the cinema), **alle otto** (at eight). It becomes **al, allo** before **il, lo** words; **alla** before **la** words, **all'** before **l'** words; **ai, agli** before **i, gli** words; **alle** before **le** words (see also page 19).

*Che cosa?/Cosa? What? **A che ora? At what time?

Asking where places are

Here and on the next two pages you can find out how to ask your way around.

Remember, in Italian there are two words for "you" -**tu** and **lei**. You say **tu** to a friend, but it is more polite to say **lei** when you are talking to an adult you don't know well.*

New words

scusi	excuse me
prego	not at all
qui	here
là/lì	over there
la posta	post office
nella piazza del mercato	in the market place
l' albergo (m)	hotel
poi	then
giri . . .	turn . . .
vada . . .	go . . .
c'è . . ?	is there . . ?
qui vicino	nearby
la via, la strada	street, road
è lontano?	is it far?
solo	only
proprio	just
a piedi	on foot
il supermercato	supermarket
di fronte a . . .	opposite . . .
la banca	bank
la farmacia	chemist's

Being polite

> *Scusi . . .*

> *Grazie.*   *Prego.*

This is how to say "Excuse me . . ."

When people thank you, it is polite to answer "**Prego**".

Where is . . ?

> *Scusi signora, dov'è la posta?*

> *Lì, proprio a fianco al supermercato.*

> *Dov'è l'albergo della stazione, per favore?*

> *Giri qui a sinistra, poi vada diritto.*

Directions

diritto

a sinistra   a destra

*You can read more about this on page 23.

Is there a ... nearby?

Is it far?

Other useful places to ask for

la stazione	una stazione di servizio	i gabinetti	una buca delle lettere
the station	a petrol station	toilets	a letter box
una cabina telefonica	un campeggio	l'ospedale	l'aeroporto
a telephone box	a campsite	the hospital	the airport

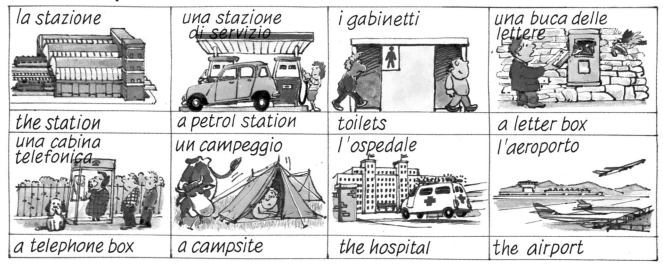

Finding your way around

Here you can find out how to ask your way around and follow directions. When you have read everything, try the map puzzle on the opposite page.

Scusi, come si va alla stazione?

Prenda la prima a destra, poi la seconda a sinistra.

La stazione è sulla destra.*

Come si va all'albergo della gioventù, per favore?

Vada diritto fino alla stazione...

Poi prenda la terza strada a destra.

Come si va all' ufficio del turismo, per favore?

In macchina? Continui diritto...

Poi prenda la prima strada a sinistra.

*Sulla destra, sulla sinistra: on the right, on the left.

New words

come si va?	how does one get to?	fino a . . .	as far as . . .
prenda . . .	take . . .	in macchina	by car
continui . . .	carry on . . .	la prima strada	the first road
l'albergo (m) della gioventù	youth hostel	la seconda	the second
		la terza	the third
l'ufficio (m) del turismo	tourist office	il Municipio	town hall
		la chiesa	church

---

prendere	to take			
io prendo	I take	**noi prendiamo**	we take	When people are telling you where to go, to be more polite they say **prenda** e.g. **Prenda la prima a destra.**
tu prendi	you take	**voi prendete**	you take (pl)	
lui/lei prende	he/she takes	**loro prendono**	they take	

Finding your way around Città di Castello

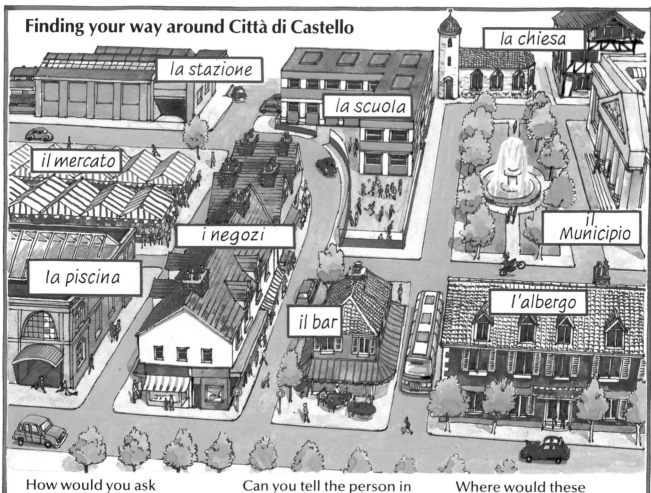

How would you ask someone the way to the market place? How would you ask them if there is a café nearby? Ask how far it is.

Can you tell the person in the yellow car how to get to the church? Can you direct someone from the hotel to the market?

Where would these directions take the yellow car? **Prenda la seconda via a sinistra, poi è sulla destra.**

Going shopping

Here and on the next two pages you can find out how to say what you want when you go shopping. When you go into an Italian shop you should say "**Buongiorno**" (during the day) or "**Buonasera**" (in the evening).

Italian money

One **Lira** is worth so little that the smallest coin is **Cinque Lire** or **L.5**. You need to remember **Cento Lire** (**L.100**) and **Mille Lire** (**L.1000**). To understand prices you must know the numbers in Italian. They are listed on page 40.

New words

fare la spesa	to go shopping
comprare	to buy
il panettiere	the baker
il negozio di alimentari	the grocer
il macellaio	the butcher
il latte	milk
l'uovo (m), le uova (f)	egg, eggs
la frutta	fruit
la verdura	vegetables
la carne	meat
il panino	bread roll
la mela	apple
il pomodoro	tomato
desidera?	can I help you?
vorrei . . .	I would like . . .
sì, certo	yes, certainly
basta così?	is that all?
nient'altro?	anything else?
quant'è /quanto costa?	how much is it?
ecco	there you are
un litro	a litre
un chilo (Kg)	a kilo
mezzo chilo	half a kilo
allora	so, well then

Signora Bonomi goes shopping

La signora Bonomi va a fare la spesa.

Compra il pane dal panettiere.

Dal panettiere

34

Compra il latte e le uova al negozio di alimentari.

Compra la frutta e la verdura al mercato.

Compra la carne dal macellaio.

Dagli alimentari

Al mercato

More shopping and going to a café

Here you can find out how to ask how much things cost and how to order things in a café.

New words

costare	to cost
quanto costa /costano?	how much is /are?
la cartolina	postcard
l'uva (f)	grapes
al chilo	. . . a kilo
l'uno/l'una	each (m/f)
la rosa	rose
me ne dà sette	give me seven
il caffè	coffee
il bar	café
il conto	bill
l'arancia (f)	orange
la banana	banana
l'ananas (m)	pineapple
il limone	lemon
la pesca	peach
la gazzosa	lemonade
la coca-cola	coca-cola
il tè	tea
con latte	with milk
un tè al limone	lemon tea
una cioccolata	hot chocolate
un bicchiere di . . .	a glass of . . .
un gelato	ice-cream

Asking how much things cost

Quanto costa questa cartolina?

Duecento Lire.

Quanto costa quell'uva?

Mille e trecento al chilo.

L.1300

Quanto costano le rose?

Settecento-cinquanta l'una.

L.750

Allora me ne dà sette.

Going to a café

Desidera?

Un caffè, per favore.

Ecco!

Grazie.

Il conto per favore.

Sono mille e cinquecento Lire.

Buying fruit

Everything on the fruit stall is marked with its name and price.

Look at the picture, then see if you can answer the questions below it.

MELE
L.1200/Kg

Desidera?

BANANE
L.2500/Kg

UVA
L.800/Kg

ARANCE
L.1800/Kg

ANANAS
L.2000 l'uno

PESCHE
L.3000/Kg

LIMONI
L. 200 l'uno

How do you tell the stallholder you would like four lemons, a kilo of bananas and a pineapple? How much do each of these things cost?

Che cosa costa duemila Lire l'uno?
Che cosa costa tremila Lire al chilo?
Che cosa costa ottocento Lire al chilo?
Che cosa costa duecento Lire?

Things to order

Here are some things you might want to order in a café.

Vorrei...

| una gazzosa | una coca-cola | un tè con latte | un tè al limone |
| una succo d'arancia | una cioccolata | un bicchiere di latte | un gelato |

The months and seasons

Here you can learn what the seasons and months are called and find out how to say what the date is.

New words

il mese	month
l'anno (m)	year
quanti ne abbiamo?	what is the date?
oggi	today
il compleanno	birthday

The seasons

la primavera	spring
l'estate (f)	summer
l'autunno (m)	autumn
l'inverno (m)	winter

The months

gennaio	January
febbraio	February
marzo	March
aprile	April
maggio	May
giugno	June
luglio	July
agosto	August
settembre	September
ottobre	October
novembre	November
dicembre	December

The seasons

la primavera

marzo, aprile, maggio

l'estate

giugno, luglio, agosto

l'autunno

settembre, ottobre, novembre

l'inverno

dicembre, gennaio, febbraio

First, second, third . . .

il primo (m)/la prima (f)	1st
il secondo/la seconda	2nd
il terzo/la terza	3rd
il quarto/la quarta	4th
il quinto/la quinta	5th
il sesto/la sesta	6th
il settimo/la settima	7th
l'ottavo/l'ottava	8th
il nono/la nona	9th
il decimo/la decima	10th

Then drop the final "i" of the number and add **esimo/a**, e.g. **undici: undicesimo** (11th).

Gennaio è il primo mese dell'anno.

Febbraio è il secondo mese dell'anno.

Dicembre è il dodicesimo mese dell'anno.

Can you say where the rest of the months come in the year?

What is the date?

Oggi è il tre maggio.

Quanti ne abbiamo oggi?

Oggi è il primo gennaio.

Writing the date

Roma, 3 maggio 1987

The date is written 1, 2, 3 … and the month (which does not take a capital letter). For "the first", you write 1, but say **il primo**.

When is your birthday?

Quand'è il tuo compleanno?

È il dieci novembre.

Il mio compleanno è il dodici febbraio.

Il compleanno di Simone è l'otto giugno.

When are their birthdays?

The dates of the children's birthdays are below their pictures. Can you say in Italian when they are, e.g. **Il compleanno di Giulia è il due aprile**.

Giulia	Massimo	Elena	Clara	Claudio	Enzo

2 aprile	21 giugno	18 ottobre	31 agosto	3 marzo	7 settembre

Colours and numbers

Colours are describing words, but only some of them change according to whether they are describing a masculine or feminine word.

The colours

rosso/a blu giallo/a verde arancione rosa nero/a bianco/a grigio/a marrone

What colour is it?

Cover the picture above and see if you can say what colour everything is in the painting. You should know all the words you need.*

Numbers

In Italian, you count the 30s to the 90s in the same way as 20-29. To count the 100s, you put the numbers 2 to 9 in front of 100. For the 1000s, you put the numbers 2 to 999 in front of 1000, but **mille** changes to **mila** (plural).

1	uno	11	undici	21	ventuno	40	quaranta
2	due	12	dodici	22	ventidue	50	cinquanta
3	tre	13	tredici	23	ventitre	60	sessanta
4	quattro	14	quattordici	24	ventiquattro	70	settanta
5	cinque	15	quindici	25	venticinque	80	ottanta
6	sei	16	sedici	26	ventisei	90	novanta
7	sette	17	diciassette	27	ventisette	100	cento
8	otto	18	diciotto	28	ventotto	200	duecento
9	nove	19	diciannove	29	ventinove	1000	mille
10	dieci	20	venti	30	trenta	2000	duemila

Pronunciation guide

In Italian, many letters are pronounced differently from the way they are said in English. The best way to learn to speak Italian is to listen carefully to Italian people and copy what they say, but here are some general points to help you.

Below is a list of letters, with a guide to how to pronounce each one. For each Italian sound we have shown part of an English word which sounds like it. Read it out loud in a normal way to find out how to pronounce the Italian sound, then practise saying the examples beneath.

a   Like the "a" sound in "car", but shorter:
Roma, amica, la, pizza

e   Like the "e" sound in "egg":
è, ecco, tetto, spaghetti

i   Like the sound "ee" in "keen", but a bit shorter:
italiano, nido, io, città, sì

o   Like the sound "o" in "odd":
io, tetto, babbo, amo

u   Like the sound "oo" in "book":
uva, cucina, tu, uno

ce, ci   "C" is soft before an "e" or "i" like the "ch" sound in "church":
ciao, uccello, cucina, mi piace

ca, co, cu   Before an "a", "o", or "u", "c" is hard like in "cake":
casa, cosa, coca-cola, scusi

che, chi   Before "he" or "hi", "c" is hard like the "k" in "kettle":
chiesa, che cosa, chiami, chi

ge, gi   "G" before an "e" or "i" is like the "j" in "jar":
gelato, mangiare, buongiorno, gennaio

ga, go, gu, gr   Before an "a", "o", "u", or "r", "g" is hard like the "g" in "game":
negozio, grazie, guardare

ghe, ghi   An "h" makes "g" hard before "e" or "i":
spaghetti

gli   Like the sound "li" in "million", with your tongue flat against the roof of your mouth:
famiglia, gli

gn   Like the sound "ni" in "onion", with your tongue flat against the roof of your mouth:
signora, signore, signorina

sce, sci   Like the sound "sh" in "shut":
piscina, pesce

h   "H" is never pronounced. "**io ho**" is pronounced "io o"

Grammar

Grammar is like a set of rules about how you put words together and it is different for every language. You will find Italian easier if you learn some of its grammar, but don't worry if you don't understand all of it straightaway. Just read a little about it at a time. This is a summary of the grammar used in this book.

Nouns

In Italian nouns are either masculine or feminine: (m) or (f). Most (m) nouns end in **o**. Most (f) nouns end in **a**. Some nouns end in **e** and are either (m) or (f).
To make the plural, you usually change the last letter to **i** for (m) nouns and **e** for (f) nouns:

	singular	plural
(m)	**albero** (tree)	**alberi** (trees)
	mobile (cupboard)	**mobili** (cupboards)
(f)	**finestra** (window)	**finestre** (windows)
	televisione	**televisioni**

The Italian for "the" often tells you whether a noun is (m) or (f).

il, lo la, l'

In the singular, "the" is

il or **lo** before (m) nouns (**il tetto, lo steccato**)
la before (f) nouns (**la finestra**)
l' before (m) and (f) nouns beginning with a vowel (**l'albero, l'insalata**).

i, gli, le

In the plural "the" becomes

i for **il** nouns (**i tetti**)
gli for **lo** and (m) **l'** nouns (**gli steccati, gli alberi**)
le before **la** and (f) **l'** nouns (**le finestre, le insalate**).

A few (m) and (f) nouns have an accent on the last vowel. These don't change in the plural: **il caffè/i caffè, la città/le città**.

al, allo, all', alla, ai, agli, alle

When **a** (at, to) is followed by **il**, they join and become **al**:

Marco è al mercato   Marco is at the market.

In the same way **a** + **lo** become **allo**:

Il gatto è a fianco allo steccato   the cat is next to the fence.

a + **la** become **alla**:

Monica è alla stazione   Monica is at the station.

a + **l'** become **all'**, **a** + **i** become **ai**, **a** + **gli** become **agli**, **a** + **le** become **alle**.

del, dello, dell', della, dei, degli, delle

When **di** (of) is followed by **il**, they join and become **del**: **il prezzo del pane**   the price of bread.

In the same way **di** + **lo** become **dello**, **di** + **l'** become **dell'**, **di** + **la** become **della**, **di** + **i** become **dei**, **di** + **gli** become **degli**, **di** + **le** become **delle**.

Del, dello etc. also mean "some", "any":

Lui mangia della carne   he is eating some meat.

Da (from) + **il** become **dal**, **da** + **lo** become **dallo** etc.
In in) + **il** become **nel**, **in** + **lo** become **nello** etc.
Su (on) + **il** become **sul**, **su** + **lo** become **sullo** etc.

un, uno, una

The word for "a/an" is **un** before **il** and masculine **l'** words, **uno** before **lo** words, **una** before **la** words and **un'** before feminine **l'** words:

un libro (m)	a book
uno strumento (m)	an instrument
una mela (f)	an apple
un'arancia (f)	an orange

My, your

The word for "my" or "your" changes depending on whether the word that follows is (m), (f), singular or plural. In Italian you usually put "the" before "my" or "your":

il mio/il tuo libro	my/your book
la mia/la tua casa	my/your house
i miei/i tuoi fratelli	my/your brothers

Adjectives

An adjective is a describing word. Italian adjectives change their endings depending on whether they are describing an (m) or (f), singular or plural word.

	singular	plural
(m)	**lui è alto** (he is tall)	**i nonni sono alti** (the grandparents are tall)
(f)	**lei è alta** (she is tall)	**le zie sono alte** (the aunts are tall)

Some adjectives end in **e** in the singular, whether (m) or (f):

Mio nonno è inglese   my grandfather is English.
Mia nonna è inglese   my grandmother is English.

These always end in **i** in the plural, whether (m) or (f):

Gli amici sono inglesi   the friends are English.
Le sorelle sono inglesi   the sisters are English.

Pronouns

When talking to one person, there are two words for "you" in Italian: **tu** and **lei**. You say **tu** to a friend and **lei** when you want to be polite or when you are talking to someone you don't know well.

Pronouns are often left out: **Mangio una mela** I eat an apple. Where in English you say "it is", in Italian you use the verb on its own: **è delizioso** it is delicious.

singular		plural	
io	I	**noi**	we
tu	you (a friend)	**voi**	you
lei	you (polite), she	**loro**	they
lui	he		

Verbs

Italian verbs (doing words) change according to who is doing the action. Most of them follow regular patterns and have the same endings. The main type of verb used in this book ends in **are**, like **mangiare** (to eat). There are some verbs in this book which do not follow this pattern, e.g. **avere**, **essere** and **andare**. It is best to learn these as you go along.

mangiare	to eat
io mangio	I eat
tu mangi	you eat (friend)
lui/lei mangia	he/she eats, you eat (polite)
noi mangiamo	we eat
voi mangiate	you eat (plural)
loro mangiano	they eat

Non

To make a verb negative in Italian, e.g. to say "I do not . . .", "he does not . . ." etc., you put **non** immediately before the verb:

Io non suono il piano   I do not play the piano.

Reflexive verbs

These are verbs which always have a special pronoun in front of them. To say "I get up" in Italian, you say "I get myself up". The pronoun changes according to who is doing the action, but **mi** always goes with **io**, **ti** with **tu** etc.

alzarsi	to get up
io mi alzo	I get up
tu ti alzi	you get up (friend)
lui/lei si alza	he/she gets up, you get up (polite)
noi ci alziamo	we get up
voi vi alzate	you get up (plural)
loro si alzano	they get up

Answers to puzzles

p.7

What are they called?
Lui si chiama Piero.
Lei si chiama Maria.
Loro si chiamano Paolo e Gianni.
Io mi chiamo . . . (your name).

Who is who?

Michele is talking to Gianni.
Anna is talking to Valeria.
Michele is next to the seal.
Gianni is talking to him.
Anna is in the bottom left-hand corner.
The man talking to Nicola is going home.

Can you remember?

Come ti chiami?
Io mi chiamo . . .
Questa è una mia amica. Si chiama Valeria.
Lui si chiama Daniele.

p.9

Can you remember?

un/il fiore, un/il gatto, un/l'albero, un/il
nido, un/l'uccello, un/il tetto, il sole, una/
la finestra, una/la macchina, un/il cane

p.11

Who comes from where?

Franz comes from Austria.
They are called Hari and Indira.
Lolita is Spanish.
Yes, Angus comes from Scotland.
Marie and Pierre come from France.
Yuri lives in Budapest.
Budapest is in Hungary.

Can you remember?

Da dove vieni?
Io vengo da . . .
Io parlo italiano.
Tu parli italiano?

p.13

How old are they?

Michele is 13.
Diana and Silvia are 15.
Giulio is 12.
Paola is 11.
Luca is 9.
Lisa is 5.

How many brothers and sisters?

A = Diana e Silvia. B = Luca. C =
Michele. D = Giulio. E = Paola.

p.17

Where is everyone?

Simone è in cucina.
Nonno è nella stanza da pranzo.
Nonna è nel soggiorno.
Mamma è nella stanza da letto.
Il fantasma è nella stanza di Isabella.
Isabella è al piano di sopra.
Piero è in bagno.

Nonno. Simone. Piero. Mamma.

Nella stanza da letto.
Nella stanza di Isabella.
Nella stanza da pranzo.
In bagno.
Nell'ingresso.

Can you remember?

Dove abiti?
Tu abiti in una casa o in un appartamento?
In campagna.
In città.
Io sono al piano di sopra.
Io sono in cucina.

p.19

Where are they hiding?

Il criceto è dentro il vaso.
Il gatto è dietro la televisione.
Il cane è dentro il mobile.

Il pappagallo è sopra lo scaffale.
Il serpente è sotto il divano.
La tartaruga è a fianco al telefono.

p.21

Who likes what?

1. Diego 2. Gianni 3. Nonno

p.23

Who is saying what?

"Ho fame."
"Buon appetito!"
"Prego, serviti."
"Mi puoi passare un bicchiere per favore?"
"Vuoi ancora patate fritte?"
"Sì grazie. Mi piacciono le patate fritte."
"No grazie. È abbastanza."
"È delizioso."

p.25

What are they doing?

A. Lui cucina. B. Lui nuota. C. Loro ballano.
D. Lei suona il violino. E. Lui dipinge.

p.27

Marco's day

1b, 2e, 3f, 4a, 5h, 6g, 7d, 8c.

What time is it?

A   Sono le tre e cinque.
B   Sono le undici e cinque.
C   Sono le nove meno dieci.
D   Sono le quattro meno un quarto.
E   Sono le tre e venticinque.
F   Sono le sette e mezza.
G   Sono le tre.
H   Sono le quattro.
I   Sono le nove.
J   È l'una e mezza.
K   Sono le sette e cinque.
L   Sono le dieci e mezza.
M   Sono le sei.
N   Sono le tre e trentacinque.
O   Sono le due meno cinque.

p.29

Venerdì sera vado a ballare con Diego.
Gioco a tennis lunedì, mercoledì e domenica.
Vado al cinema mercoledì sera.
Martedì.
Domenica gioco a tennis.
La festa è alle sette.

p.33

Scusi, come si va al mercato?
Scusi, c'è un bar qui vicino?
È lontano?

Prenda la terza strada a sinistra, poi
diritto.

Prenda la terza a destra poi diritto. Il
mercato è sulla sinistra.
To the school.

p.37

Vorrei quattro limoni, un chilo di banane
e un ananas, per favore.
Duecento Lire l'uno.
Duemila e cinquecento Lire al chilo.
Duemila Lire l'uno.
un ananas. le pesche. l'uva. un limone.

p.39

Il compleanno di Giulia è il due aprile.
Il compleanno di Massimo è il ventuno
giugno.
Il compleanno di Elena è il diciotto ottobre.
Il compleanno di Clara è il trentuno agosto.
Il compleanno di Claudio è il tre marzo.
Il compleanno di Enzo è il sette settembre.

p.40

La strada è grigia.
Il sole è giallo.
Il tetto è arancione.
Il cielo è blu.
I fiori sono rosa.
Il cane è marrone.
L'uccello è nero.
La macchina è rossa.
Gli alberi sono verdi.
La casa è bianca.

Glossary

Adjectives and pronouns are shown in their masculine singular form. Irregular plurals of nouns are shown in brackets next to the letters "pl".

a	at, to
a fianco a	next to
a piedi	on foot
abbastanza	enough, sufficient
abitare	to live
l'acqua (f)	water
l'aeroporto (m)	airport
affettuoso	friendly
agosto	August
l'albergo (m)	hotel
l'albergo della gioventù (m)	youth hostel
l'albero (m)	tree
gli alimentari	groceries, grocery shop
allora	then
alto	tall
altrettanto	the same to you (answer to "buon appetito")
altro	more, anything else, other
alzarsi	to get up
amare	to love
l'amburgher (m)	hamburger
l'amico/l'amica	friend (m/f)
l'ananas (m) (pl. gli ananas)	pineapple
anche	also, too
ancora	more
andare	to go
l'anno (m)	year
l'appartamento (m)	flat
aprile	April
l'arancia (f)	orange (fruit)
arancione (m/f)	orange (colour)
l'armadio (m)	wardrobe
arrivederci	Goodbye
ascoltare	to listen to
l'autunno (m)	autumn
l'Austria (f)	Austria
avere	to have
aver fame	to be hungry
il babbo	Dad
il bagno	bath, bathroom
ballare	to dance
la banana	banana
la banca	bank
il bar	café
basso	short (of height)
basta così?	is that all?
bene	well
bianco	white
il bicchiere	glass (for drinking)
biondo	blond
blu	blue
la buca delle lettere	post box
buon appetito	Enjoy your meal!
buonasera	Good Evening
buongiorno	Hello, Good Day

buono	good
il burro	butter
la cabina telefonica	phone box
il caffè	coffee
il calcio	football
la campagna	countryside
il campeggio	campsite
il cane	dog
la carne	meat
la cartolina	postcard
la casa	house
castano	chestnut (brown)
il castello	castle
c'è	there is
la cena	supper, evening meal
cercare	to look for
certo	certainly
che cosa?	what?
che ore sono?	what time is it?
che peccato!	what a pity!
chi?	who?
la chiesa	church
il chilo	kilo
ci vediamo	see you . . .
il cinema	cinema
ciao	Hello/Goodbye
la cioccolata	chocolate
la città	city, town
la coca-cola	coca-cola
la colazione	breakfast
come stai?	how are you?
come ti chiami?	what is your name?
il comignolo	chimney
il compleanno	birthday
comprare	to buy
continuare	to continue
il conto	bill
cosa?	what?
costare	to cost
il criceto	hamster
la crostata di frutta	fruit tart
la cucina	kitchen
cucinare	to cook
da	from
dare	to give
davanti a	in front of
delizioso	delicious
dentro	inside
desiderare	to wish
dicembre	December
dietro	behind
di fronte a	opposite
dipingere	to paint
di più	more
il divano	sofa
domani	tomorrow
la domenica	Sunday
dove	where
e	and
ecco	there is, here is
eccolo/a	there he, it/she, it is
essere	to be
l'estate (f)	summer

la famiglia	family	la madre	mother
la fame	hunger	maggio	May
il fantasma	ghost	magro	thin
fare	to do/make	male	badly, unwell
fare colazione	to have breakfast	mamma	Mum
fare la spesa	to go shopping (for food)	mangiare	to eat
la farmacia	chemist's	marrone	brown
febbraio	February	il martedì	Tuesday
la festa	party	marzo	March
la finestra	window	la mattina (or il mattino)	morning
fino a	as far as	la mela	apple
il fiore	flower	il mercato	market
il formaggio	cheese	il mercoledì	Wednesday
la Francia	France	il mese	month
il fratello	brother	la mezzanotte	midnight
la frutta	fruit	il mezzogiorno	midday
		mezzo	half
il gabinetto	toilet	mi	me, myself
il garage (pl. i garage)	garage	mio	my, mine
il gatto	cat	mi piace	I like
la gazzosa	lemonade	il mobile	cupboard
il gelato	ice cream	il modellismo	model-building
i genitori	parents	molto	a lot, much, very
gennaio	January	il municipio	town hall
la Germania	Germany	la musica	music
giallo	yellow		
giocare	to play	né	neither, nor
giovane (m/f) (pl. giovani)	young	il negozio	shop
il giovedì	Thursday	nero	black
girare	to turn	nessun(o)/a	not any (m/f)
giugno	June	il nido	nest
grasso	fat	niente	nothing
grazie	thank you	nient'altro?	anything else?
grigio	grey	no	no
guardare	to look	non . . . affatto	not at all
		la nonna	grandmother
in	in	il nonno	grandfather
l'India (f)	India	novembre	November
l'Inghilterra (f)	England	nuotare	to swim
inglese	English	nuovo	new
l'inglese (m)	English language		
l'ingresso (m)	entrance, hall	o	or
l'insalata (f)	salad	oggi	today
l'inverno (m)	winter	l'ospedale (m)	hospital
l'Italia (f)	Italy	ottobre	October
italiano	Italian		
l'italiano (m)	Italian language	il padre	father
		il pane	bread
là, lì	over there	il panettiere	baker
il latte	milk	il panificio	baker's
lavorare	to work	il panino	bread roll
lavorare a maglia	to knit	papà	Dad
leggere	to read	il pappagallo	parrot
il letto	bed	parlare	to speak
il limone	lemon	le patate fritte	chips
la Lira	Lira (Italian money)	passare	to pass
il litro	litre	la pesca	peach
lontano	far	il pesce	fish
luglio	July	il piano di sopra	upstairs
il lunedì	Monday	la pianta	plant
		il pianoforte	piano
ma	but	la piazza	square
il macellaio	butcher	la piscina	swimming pool
la macelleria	butcher's	la pizza	pizza
la macchina	car	un poco	a little

poi	then, after
la poltrona	armchair
il pomeriggio	afternoon
il pomodoro	tomato
la porta	door
la posta	post office
il pranzo	lunch
prego	not at all (answer to "grazie")
preferire	to prefer
prendere	to take
presto	soon
la primavera	spring
primo	first
pronto	ready
proprio	just
il prosciutto	ham
qualcosa	something
quando?	when?
quanti?	how many?
quanti ne abbiamo?	what is the date?
quanto?	how much?
quarto	fourth, quarter
quasi	almost
questo, quello	this, that
qui	here
il riso	rice
in riva al mare	by the sea
rosa	pink
la rosa	rose
rosso	red
il sabato	Saturday
la salsiccia	sausage
lo scaffale	shelf
la Scozia	Scotland
la scuola	school
scusi	excuse me
secondo	second
la sera	evening
il serpente	snake
serviti	help yourself
settembre	September
sì	yes
signora	madam, Mrs.
signore	Sir, Mr.
signorina	Miss
il sole	sun
solo	only, alone
il soggiorno	living room
sopra	above, on
soprattutto	above all
la sorella	sister
sotto	under
gli spaghetti (pl)	spaghetti
la Spagna	Spain
lo sport (pl. gli sport)	sport

la stanza	room
la stanza da letto	bedroom
la stanza da pranzo	dining room
stare bene	to be well
stasera	tonight, this evening
la stazione	station
la stazione di servizio	petrol station
lo steccato	fence
la strada	road
lo strumento musicale	musical instrument
su	on, over
sulla destra/sinistra	on the right/left
il succo	juice
suonare	to play music
il supermercato	supermarket
il tappeto	carpet
la tartaruga	tortoise
la tavola	table
il tè	tea
tedesco	German
il tedesco	German language
il telefono	telephone
la televisione	television
il tempo libero	spare time
la tenda	curtain
il tennis	tennis
terzo	third
il tetto	roof
ti	yourself
la torta	cake
tra	between
trovare	to find
tuo	your, yours
l'uccello (m)	bird
l'ufficio del turismo (m)	tourist office
un, una, uno	a, an
l'Ungheria (f)	Hungary
l'uno/l'una (m/f)	each
l'uovo (m) (pl. le uova, f)	egg
l'uva (f)	grapes
va bene	all is well, O.K.
il vaso	vase
vecchio	old
il venerdì	Friday
venire	to come
verde	green
la verdura	vegetables
verso	towards
la via	street
vicino	near
il violino	violin
volere	to want
la zia	aunt
lo zio	uncle

First published in 1987 by Usborne Publishing Ltd.
Usborne House, 83-85 Saffron Hill
London EC1N 8RT, England.
Copyright © 1987 Usborne Publishing Ltd.

Printed in Great Britain.